Whispers from a cloud. "The Rise of a Warrior"

Tina Calleri

Table of Contents

Prologue

I was three years old when I first looked out the window of an airplane and saw the face of God in a cloud.

To some, it may sound like the imagination of a child. But for me, that moment marked the beginning of a lifelong search—for safety, for meaning, for love, and above all, for strength. I didn't know it then, but that cloud would become a symbol I'd return to many times throughout my life. In moments of joy and devastation, in silence and survival, I would look up and search for that face.

I have lived a life that many would find hard to believe—one filled with beauty and brutality, love and betrayal, silence and song. I was a daughter, a sister, a child caretaker, a wife, a mother, and—eventually—a survivor. I was told to stay quiet. I was taught to obey. I was expected to sacrifice. And for a long time, I did.

But there comes a moment when silence becomes too loud to bear. When fear turns into fire. When the woman finally broke free from the chains of cultural bondage, she awakened to the truth of who she was— strong, worthy, and no longer afraid to live life on her own terms.

This book is that remembrance.

It is not just a recounting of events—it is a resurrection. Of the girl whose dreams were taken. Of the woman who fought to protect her children. Of the voice that refused to be buried any longer.

To those who feel alone in their pain, to the ones silenced by fear or shame—this story is for you. I share it not because it's easy, but because it's necessary. Because if even one reader sees their own strength reflected in these pages, then every scar I carry will have served a greater purpose.

I am Tina Calleri.

And this is how I found my way back to the girl who believed God was in the clouds—only to discover, He had placed the strength within me all along.

Dedication

To all the women who have faced the trials of resilience and adversity, navigating the constraints of cultural beliefs that have shaped our lives since childhood. We have stood in this position for far too long, burdened by fear and the weight of tradition that instilled doubt in our hearts. This story is for those of us who have struggled to break free from the bondage of culture, questioning why it took us so long to shed the fears that held us captive. May we find strength in our shared experiences, and may we inspire one another to overcome our challenges and pursue the lives we truly desire. Together, let us continue to empower ourselves and each other in the journey towards liberation.

A long time ago, I vividly remember a day when I was just three years old—back in July of 1959. My mother and I were flying on an airplane from Italy to Canada. As I gazed out the window, I became mesmerized by the fluffy clouds drifting below us. One cloud, in particular, captured my eyes—it looked like a design of an old man face with eyes, a nose, ears, and a mouth, with wild long hair and a long, flowing beard.

So high above the earth, I recalled my mother telling me that God lived in heaven, far up in the sky. In my innocent little mind, I imagined and believed that this cloud with a face was God Himself. From that day forward, I always imagined God looking like that whimsical cloud. And whenever I looked up at the sky, I searched for that familiar face. Though I never saw it again, I never stopped looking.

Even at the tender age of three, I was incredibly close to my mother—I called her my best friend. She was everything to me. Whenever I had a question, she would look deep into my eyes and give me an answer—whether it was true or not. I believed every word she said. Only later in life did I come to understand that many of her answers were stories she had created—beautiful, comforting tales to fill the emptiness left by her own childhood.

In 1959, my mother and I immigrated to Canada, where my father had already settled and was building a future for our family. As newcomers in a strange country, we lived in a house shared with five other families—my father's brothers, their wives, and children. It was a crowded, chaotic life, and one of the main reasons both my parents worked tirelessly—just to cover expenses, survive, and save for a place of their own.

Two years later, their hard work paid off—they purchased a house, fulfilling their dream.

At the age of five, I began kindergarten, a chapter that filled me with fear. Not knowing a word of English made the experience even more intimidating. On top of that, I was ridiculed by my classmates, who cruelly called me "chocolate face" because of the color of my skin. Their words cut deeply and made the idea of going to school terrifying.

Yet I had no choice but to press on. Slowly, I learned English and began to find my voice. With each new word, I uncovered a strength I didn't know I had—the strength to stand up for myself. I developed ways to protect myself from the bullying, and over time, I transformed fear into resilience. Even at just five years old, I was learning how to turn pain into power and struggles into wisdom and stepping stones.

Eventually, I started to make friends. Recess became a time of laughter, and the support of new companions helped me rebuild my confidence, one moment at a time.

As the years passed, I thrived academically. I excelled in school and achieved remarkable success. I still remember the day I was told I'd be receiving a special award—one of only ten students in my class to be honored at a ceremony in the school auditorium. Parents were invited to attend, to witness and celebrate their children's achievements. I was overjoyed. As soon as I got home, I ran to my parents, eyes sparkling with excitement, and told them, *"You have to be there. It would mean everything to me."*

They smiled and made a promise. *"Of course, we'll be there."* And I believed them—completely. I held onto that promise with the wide-eyed trust only a child can give so freely.

But when the big day arrived, and my name was called, I walked up to the stage with trembling hands and a heart full of joy. I stood there looking around the auditorium, scanning the sea of faces for the two people I wanted to see most and I finally realized that my two seats were empty.

Imagined how I felt as a little girl watching other students beam as their parents cheered them on. Once again, I found myself navigating both the highs and lows of life on my own.

I blinked away the tears and forced a smile as I accepted my award, my heart quietly breaking beneath the applause. When I got home that evening, I was furious with my parents. I asked them, at the dinner table, *"Why didn't you come? You promised."*

Their response was simple, but it pierced deeper than they could know. They were too afraid to ask for time off. They thought missing work might cost them their jobs that is why they didn't show up. They chose their livelihood over my moment.

At just seven years old, I was left with a painful realization: that their work, their fears, their responsibilities—those came before me. That moment etched itself into my heart, planting a belief that would take years to unlearn—that maybe I wasn't as important as I thought I was... or hoped to be.

By the age of ten, I had a five-year-old brother and a newborn baby sister. Just three months after giving birth, my mother returned to work. With both my parents working full-time, I had no choice to become the caretaker of my younger siblings. Imagine the weight of that responsibility on such small little shoulders—following adult instructions, managing two little lives, and my own, striving to meet my parents' expectations so they wouldn't be disappointed when they came home. As fear was a constant companion. I made sure the house was clean, the beds were made, and my brother and sister were safe and fed—all while still attending school and trying to learn.

During the 1960s, the image of the perfect life was a house with a garage, two kids, and a dog. My parents had everything except the dog. From the outside, it seemed like we were living the dream. But inside, I felt like I was missing out. I carried out adult responsibilities, did chores, went to school, and took care of my siblings. My childhood was slipping away. Though I didn't express it at the time, I harbored deep resentment—anger that I now understand was rooted in my fear of hurting my parents. Even as a child, I knew they were doing their best. That awareness shaped me into a people-pleaser—always trying to make others happy, often using humor and laughter to mask my own pain.

Despite the challenges, I was blessed with a God-given gift: a beautiful singing voice. Music became my escape, my sanctuary. My mother recognized my passion and often had me sing for family and friends. Her brothers were musicians and played in a wedding band, and I would tag along and perform on stage. I loved being in the spotlight—something I rarely experienced at home. On stage, I felt alive. I felt seen. I felt free, I felt heard.

When I was twelve, an opportunity of a lifetime came my way. A popular Italian television show, *Carasello Italiano*, was auditioning children with talent, and my mother submitted my name. To my amazement, I was selected to perform on TV. During the show, I met a well-known couple from the Italian community who were so impressed with my voice that they offered to manage my career in New York City.

But my parents said no—firmly and without discussion. My father believed that for a girl to succeed in show business, she would have to sacrifice her integrity to managers and producers. At twelve, I had no voice in the decision. A dream that felt within reach slipped through my fingers, and a piece of me shattered. For a long time, I resented my father for making that choice for me. Later in life, I asked him, "Why did you say no? That opportunity could've changed my life." He simply said, "You were too young. A girl's place is to be at home and with her family." My father, unaware of how much singing meant to me, dismissed it without a second thought—never understanding that in doing so, he was dimming the very light that made me feel alive.

Growing up, I often felt the heavy burden of being a girl in our culture. Boys had freedom. Girls had rules. They were expected to obey, to conform, to please. I witnessed this disparity even within my own family. My father's favoritism towards my brother was undeniable—and hurtful.

I remember one particular moment when I was thirteen. I longed for a bicycle, and after begging my father, he finally came home with one. My heart raced with excitement—until he called my brother over and handed the bike to him. He insisted it was for all of us, but his gesture spoke volumes. I was devastated. Tears welled up in my eyes "You're too old to be riding a bike," he said, waving it off. "Don't be silly—stop crying."

My mother, ever intuitive, saw the pain in my eyes. She knew how deeply that moment wounded me.

But in that heartbreak, I made a quiet decision. I claimed that bike as mine. I rode it everywhere. With the wind in my face and joy in my heart, I embraced the rare feeling of freedom. For once, I felt like a child— laughing, pedaling, soaring. That simple act of defiance ignited a flame inside me. It reminded me that I could choose joy, even when joy wasn't handed to me.

Looking back, it saddens me to think how much I gave up as the firstborn daughter. I was molded into an adult long before my time. I wasn't allowed to dream freely or even enjoy the innocence of riding a bike without earning it or competing for it. Every victory felt like a struggle, every joy a fight.

My mother tried to fill the emptiness I felt by sewing me beautiful clothes and choosing the finest outfits, knowing how much I cherished fashion and the confidence it gave me. She could see the sadness in my eyes and understood the hurt I carried within. In time, I came to learn about the struggles she had endured as the eldest daughter in her family. Without realizing it, she had passed much of her pain onto me. Like many women of her generation, she had been shaped by the cultural beliefs and traditions that governed her world—and those same beliefs were passed down to me.

Life went on. By the ages of thirteen and fourteen, I was still the caretaker for my younger siblings whenever our parents were working. But I had also stepped into a new role: that of an advocate for my parents. I became their voice, their interpreter, and their guide through a world they didn't yet understand. I translated conversations from Italian to English and back again—at doctor's appointments, during meetings with lawyers, when negotiating mortgage deals, and even on everyday phone calls. I read their mail and explained its contents, helping them navigate the complexities of adult life in a new country.

At a time when most thirteen-year-olds were navigating the halls of middle school and learning about themselves, I was shouldering the responsibilities of a grown woman. I had no choice but to mature quickly, confronting the trials, pressures, and stress of adulthood far too soon.

By sixteen, though, everything seemed to change for the better. I loved school—I was an honor student, an athlete full of energy and drive. I had a part-time job, a circle of great friends, and my parents were finally financially stable. We lived in a beautiful neighborhood, in a house framed by a white picket fence and blooming roses. We were living the Canadian Dream, and I knew just how much my parents had sacrificed to get us there.

We were healthy, happy, and full of hope. I admired my parents deeply because I had witnessed firsthand the hardships they had endured to give us this life. I felt nothing but love and gratitude for them.

Everything seemed perfect—but in 1972, when I was just sixteen, a single moment changed the course of my life forever.

One afternoon while visiting relatives, I met a tall, handsome young man who had just arrived from Italy. His captivating blue eyes immediately drew me in. He was 21 years old who had recently completed two years in the Italian Marines and looked every bit the gentleman in his crisp white uniform. We struck up a conversation and instantly clicked. We exchanged phone numbers and began talking for hours each day. We even started secretly meeting whenever we could.

After six months of courting me, he asked my parents for my hand in marriage. My father—strong-willed and protective—immediately refused. "No way! She's only sixteen! *Ma chi si pazzu?*" he shouted. ("Are you crazy?")

But I was young and hopelessly in love. I challenged my father's decision like never before. Surprisingly, he gave in—a rare and unexpected reversal. Only later did I learn the reason behind his change of heart: he was afraid I would run away with this man and bring shame to the family.

So, we got engaged and began planning the wedding. Two weeks before the church ceremony, we quietly married at City Hall.

That same day, on the bus ride home, everything changed.

He began flirting with other women, laughing and joking as if I didn't exist. Jealousy bubbled up inside me, and I gently nudged him with my elbow and whispered, "Stop it."

What happened next shattered me.

He turned toward me and, without warning, slapped me across the face. I was stunned. Silent. Tears streamed down my cheek as I cradled my face in disbelief. He leaned in close, his voice low and threatening.

"I'm your husband now. You do what I say—when I say, and how. You keep your mouth shut and never embarrass me again."

After we got off the bus, I swung my purse at him and shouted that I never wanted to see him again. Then I ran home as fast as I could. That night, I tearfully told my parents what had happened and that I no longer wanted to marry him. They were devastated. My mother cried as she held me, and my father erupted in rage, yelling, "I'm going to kill him! I'll spend the rest of my life in jail!"

My mother began to panic, pulling at her hair and clutching her chest claiming she was having a heart attack. "You're legally married now! The church wedding is in two weeks—what are we going to do? The invitations have been sent! What will people say?" Both of my parents went into panic mode.

No one asked how I felt. No one acknowledged my pain. It was as if my voice had been erased from the conversation. I felt blamed—as if I had ruined everything—when in reality, I was the one who had been hurt. I was the victim, but I had no space to be heard.

That same night, he came to our house in tears. He apologized profusely to both me and my parents. He used his charm and played the victim well, promising that it would never happen again. I felt overwhelmed and trapped—just sixteen years old, caught between my parents' fears and my own.

And just like that, it was swept under the rug, as if it had never happened.

Then came the church wedding day.

As I walked down the aisle, my eyes filled with tears—carrying a fear I couldn't explain, but one that gripped me with every step. It was supposed to be the happiest day of my life, but with each stride toward the altar, the confusion deepened—I knew in my heart this wasn't right, yet I kept moving forward. That day I sealed a vow I was not sure of just to ease my parent's fears.

Months later, we were living in an upstairs flat in my parents' house. I was three months pregnant when we got into a heated argument. He grabbed me by the hair, dragged me down the stairs, and threw me to the ground. Then he climbed on top of me and beat me—viciously, relentlessly. I begged him to stop. He finally left, slamming the door behind him, and drove off, leaving me there—battered, bleeding, and I was afraid I might lose my baby.

I lay on the floor with two black eyes, my face swollen and bruised in every shade imaginable. My lip was split and bleeding. My entire body trembled. I was terrified—not only for myself but for the life growing inside me.

As I lay there, struggling to keep my swollen eyes open, I looked up at the ceiling—and there it was the image of the same cloud I had seen when I was just three years old, flying above the sky. That familiar, comforting shape—the one I thought was the face of God.

In that moment of vulnerability, I shouted through my sobs, "God, please help me."

I dragged my aching body to a nearby chair, clutching my stomach, praying with everything in me that my baby was okay.

Later that evening my parents arrived home, my seven-year-old sister Sylvia came upstairs to check on me. The moment she saw my face, she froze in fear and let out a scream. She ran down the stairs quickly sobbing, shouting for my parents. When they came up and saw me, they were horrified. My father turned ghostly white. My mother collapsed into tears, screaming, "My daughter, what has he done to her?"

It took everything in us to hold my father back. He was determined to find him—to make him pay.

We called the police and reported the assault. Officers escorted me to the hospital to make sure the baby and I were okay. Thank God, my baby was unharmed.

But in the 1970s, domestic violence wasn't treated with the gravity it deserves. The police told me to go to court and file a complaint, but I didn't. I was terrified—afraid of what he'd do if he found out. I was still hiding my truth, still brushing the pain under the rug, still haunted by that familiar phrase:

"What will people think?"

One night, we were driving home from a party in Niagara Falls when we were rear-ended. An officer arrived and advised us not to drive the car—it wasn't safe. But the moment the officer left, my husband insisted we get back in and drive home.

I refused. I wouldn't risk my life or my one-year-old son's. I stood my ground.

He threatened to leave us there. I thought he was bluffing.

He wasn't.

He got in the car and drove off, leaving me alone on a dark, rural road in the middle of nowhere a farmland—with no streetlights, no traffic, and a baby in my arms.

Terrified, heart pounding, and holding a crying baby in my arms. I scanned the area and saw a small farmhouse in the distance with a light on. I gathered what courage I had left and began walking up the long dark gravel path to the front door.

An older couple opened the door, concern etched across their faces. "Are you okay?" they asked.

They let me in to use their phone. I called my parents, who were still at the party. They came right away and brought us safely home.

On the drive home, all I could hear was my father repeating his go-to phrase: "I'm going to kill him." My mother, equally furious, kept asking, "How could he do this to you—and to your child?"

When we reached home, I begged my father to stay in the car. I could see the rage building in his eyes, and I feared what might happen if he went inside. Thankfully, my parents respected my wishes and simply dropped me off at the door.

When I stepped inside there he was with a furious look on his face, and waiting for me with a belt clenched in his hand, fury etched across his face.

I rushed upstairs to put my son to bed, but before I could make it to the bathroom to lock the door, he grabbed me. What happened next is what you're probably already imagining.

Years passed.

I kept the abuse hidden from everyone—my family, my friends, my coworkers. I was ashamed. I wore long-sleeved sweaters in the middle of summer to cover the bruises on my arms. I hid my swollen face under makeup. And if the marks were still visible, I'd invent some excuse—"I tripped," "I hit my face on the cupboard," "I fell."

I became an expert at pretending living a happy life and I was really good at it.

I was 35 years old now—with three children—and this nightmare still hadn't ended. He did whatever he wanted. Came home whenever he pleased. I stayed silent to avoid confrontation. I lived under the heavy blanket of fear.

Then one Saturday night, curiosity got the better of me. I had discovered where he usually went out, and I decided to see for myself. I drove to a nightclub—and there he was. Laughing, dancing, having the time of his life—with a woman who happened to be a friend of mine.

When he spotted me, he stormed over, grabbed me, dragged me into the lobby, and slapped me so hard I thought my neck snapped.

Tears filled my eyes. But this time, something inside me lit up.

I looked him dead in the eye and said, *"You're going to pay for this."* And I walked away.

That night, standing in front of the mirror, I saw the handprint on my cheek—and something inside me broke. Or maybe it finally healed. I stared at myself and asked:

"Why am I still putting up with this? Why am I staying in this marriage of terror?"

And then I screamed at myself—**"What's wrong with you? Where's the Tina who was a leader in school? The athlete with drive? The bank employee juggling serious responsibilities? The girl who raised her siblings before she even hit her teens? Tina, if you don't fight... you'll never win, (The moment of truth) Stand up for yourself!"**

So I did.

"I put my armor on, I'll show you who I am.
I'm unstoppable. I'm a Porsche with no brakes.
I'm invincible. I'll win every single game."

The very next day, I filed for divorce. The weight of seventeen years lifted off my shoulders the moment I signed the papers.

He was served. It was official.

One day, I went to the house while he was at work. I walked into the kitchen and found our wedding album—stabbed through with a butcher knife. The wedding video was shredded. All our family photos had been burned in the fireplace. My organ piano was smashed to pieces.

I packed a few belongings. My kids were waiting in the car. But just as I was getting ready to leave, he came home and blocked the driveway.

When I refused to get out of the car, he grabbed a crowbar and smashed the windows. My children were in the backseat, huddled together, glass flying around them. Then he slashed the tires with a knife.

I managed to get the kids out and ran with them into the laundry room. We locked the door behind us. With my voice shaking, I dialed 911.

They heard the fear in my voice. The SWAT team arrived.

He was arrested. He served jail time. A restraining order was issued. He was banned from returning to the house.

For a while, things were quiet.

Then one Sunday morning, as I was making breakfast, there was a knock at the door. My daughter answered—and he barged in.

I reminded him of the restraining order. I held back from calling the police, only because my children were present. I didn't want to further traumatize them.

As we argued, I waved my arms in frustration—and a butter knife slipped from my hand, landing near his feet and at the same time I turned, picked up the phone, and said firmly, *"Leave, or I'm calling 911."*

He left.

Two hours later, the police were at my door.

"Are you Tina Calleri?" one of them asked.

"Yes, sir, I am."

Without warning, they grabbed me, handcuffed me, and threw me to the ground.

"You're under arrest," the officer said.

"What the hell?! Why?" I screamed.

They wouldn't answer. They read me my rights and escorted me out.

As they led me to the police car, I looked back at my children—crying, screaming, "Mama! Mama!"

My youngest daughter, just ten years old, was on her knees, pleading with the officers not to take me away.

My heart shattered.

That man—the same one with a restraining order—had taken the butter knife to the police and claimed I had threw it at him. My fingerprints were, of course, on it. That was all they needed.

I tried to explain the truth, that he wasn't even supposed to be there.

But the officer simply said, *"Ma'am, you should've called 911."*

And then they threw me in jail.

I couldn't believe how quickly my day had unraveled—from making breakfast for my kids to sitting in a jail cell beside prostitutes and drug dealers. It was a nightmare I'll never forget. I remember thinking, *"Who would've ever imagined this would be my reality?"*

The next day, I stood before a judge and told my story. He was furious. Looking directly at my husband, he called him "the scum of the earth" and ordered him out of the courtroom. My husband bolted like a coward—with his tail between his legs—faster than I could say, *"Ma vaffanculo, bastardo!"*

All charges against me were dropped.

Though the divorce process was still underway, the court ordered him to pay child and spousal support. He never did.

But he underestimated me.

I placed a writ of seizure on the house. I garnished his wages. I presented evidence to the motor vehicle department and proved to them that he was a deadly father which blocked him from renewing his license and license plate registration. I sued the York Region Police Department for defamation of character—and I won, including a monetary settlement. I made sure the truth came to light. I made sure people knew the monster behind the mask.

Eventually, the matrimonial home was sold. I purchased a new house and built a peaceful environment for my children. And would you believe he bought a house just around the corner—trying to intimidate me, to spy, to control.

But I had gained power he could no longer touch.

Once he realized that, he sold the house and disappeared.

I raised my children as a single mother. He remained absent from their lives for many years. My parents became my strongest allies. They were my rocks in the darkest hours—especially my mother, who gave me the emotional foundation I needed to keep going.

My father loved me deeply, but his protective nature often led him to control. His fears were rooted in old beliefs and social pressure. He warned me that dating again could destroy my reputation in our Italian community.

"Don't bring shame to our family name. People talk."
"You'll be branded the biggest whore in town."

Those words stayed with me, embedded in my mind like barbed wire. Even as I broke free from cultural bondage, part of me still wrestled with the fear he planted in me.

But despite the conflict between my desires and my upbringing, I pressed forward. I prioritized the safety and happiness of my children above all. And yes—I found love again. Quietly at first. I wanted it to be grounded in peace before I shared it with the world. One day, I'll tell that part of the story too.

I worked tirelessly to support my family—like that old Dolly Parton song says:
"Working nine to five, what a way to make a living,
Barely getting by, it's all taking and no giving…"

Then, just when I thought I had created stability, life threw me another curveball. I lost my job. I collapsed into despair, curled up for days, crying under the crushing weight of uncertainty.

Then one night, I heard a news report about a daycare shortage in Ontario. At the time, I was babysitting my nephew—and something inside me sparked.

"What if I watch a few more kids? I could make a decent weekly income."

So I took a leap of faith and placed a small ad in the *Markham Economist*.

I forgot all about it—until the phone started ringing nonstop.

Thank God I have the gift of gab! Before I knew it, I was running a home daycare. I embraced the role of entrepreneur, earned my Early Childhood Education certificate, hired staff as the daycare grew, and today—32 years later—I still welcome families through my doors, helping to shape the little architects of our future.

My children are grown now, married with families of their own. I am the proud grandmother of six beautiful grandchildren—the loves of my life.

My journey hasn't been easy. But it's been rich with lessons. I often reflect on why it took me so long to leave the abuse and why I hesitated to fight back.

It all came down to fear—fear of disgrace, fear of judgment, fear of what people would say.

At sixteen, I was married and taught to obey. I was conditioned to remain silent. To pretend. I was led to believe that a husband ruled the household, and if he hit you—you endured it. You never pushed back.

But that little girl grew into a woman who would no longer stay silent.

That woman fought back—and she won.

I stopped caring about what my name meant to others. I wanted freedom for myself. For my children. I broke the cultural chains that had bound me.

That little girl—forced to grow up at ten, silenced by fear, whose singing dreams were stolen—**she rose.**
She found her voice.
She claimed her power.

I transformed pain into strength. I turned trauma into wisdom. I faced legal battles, abuse, betrayal, false accusations—even jail time. But I stood tall. And I overcame.

Sometimes, those memories still sneak out of my eyes and roll down my cheeks. The pain may remain, but it no longer controls me.

Today, when people ask me, *"How are you, Tina?"*
I smile and say, *"I'm happy."*

I've reclaimed my joy. I sing again—at events, at celebrations, in worship. I share my knowledge, my truth, and my faith. I couldn't have done this without believing in myself... and knowing that **God has always been my biggest cheerleader.**

Through the darkest nights, His light guided me. His presence reminded me of who I was:

In God, I found my worth.
In God, I found my identity.
And yes—I believe.
This ends with me.

As I stand here today, I reflect on the incredible journey that led me here. Every trial, every tear, every fear shaped me into the woman I am now— resilient, empowered, whole. I've learned that resilience is born through fire and that every setback is a setup for a comeback.

When I look at my children and the lives they're building, I feel immense pride. I didn't just break the cycle of abuse—I carved out a new path for them. A path built on love, respect, and the belief that they are worthy. I've made it my mission to teach them the power of self-worth—and the courage it takes to speak out.

It's my passion to help others who feel voiceless. To show them they are not alone. That there is always a way out. I often think of that little girl, staring up at the clouds, searching for the face of God.

And now I know—
That strength I was looking for?
It was always within me.

Today, as I continue to sing, to speak, and to share, I do so with purpose. Music has always been my way of expressing emotions—of reaching people's hearts. Whether through joyful melodies or soul-stirring ballads, I use my voice to uplift and inspire.

And I cherish the relationships I've built along the way—my friends, my family, my support system. They've been my shelter in the storm, celebrating every small victory with me.

I'm no longer defined by what I've endured.
I'm defined by how I rose.

I've learned to embrace my scars—they're not signs of damage, but symbols of survival.

Looking ahead, I dream of creating a safe haven for women and children who've experienced abuse. A place where they can find shelter, support, and belonging. A reminder that **your past does not dictate your future.** You can reclaim your joy—no matter how long it takes.

From a little girl at three, to the woman I am today—
I am a survivor.
A mother.
A singer.
A warrior.

I will continue to fight for those who cannot fight for themselves. I will speak truth, break silence, and shatter the cycles of abuse woven into cultural expectations.

Thank you for allowing me to share my story. Your support means the world to me.

Together, we can build a future where love and respect are the norm—
Where every child can dream without fear.

Let this be a reminder:
We all have the power to rewrite our stories,
to rise above our past,
and to shine brightly—
in a world that too often tries to dim our light.

Thank you.

A Final Whisper

This Ends With Me

A little girl in a plane high above, a child gazes wide,

Fluffy clouds below, where dreams reside.

A cloud shaped like a face I thought was God ,

A whisper of hope, in the sky so bold.

Wisdom of hope untold

"God's up in heaven," mother's voice said,

Innocence blooming, as imagination spread.

That cloud was a guide, in the sky so blue,

A search for a face forever I pursued.

From Italy's shores to Canada's land,

A journey commenced, with my mamma hand in hand.

In a house of many, where dreams tangled tight,

My Parents worked hard, and day turned to night.

School days were tough, taunts cut like knives,

"Chocolate face" I was called e, but I learned to strive.

With every heartbeat, resilience did grow,

Transforming my fears into strength from woe.

I learned to persist, in the face of disdain,

Finding friends at recess, joy took away pain.

As years rolled on, I danced through the halls,

With awards and triumphs, I answered the calls.

The shadows of a young girl loomed heavy ,and burdens I bore,

I was caretaker for my siblings ', I was , an advocate for my parents and I was needed for more,

Among all the chaos, I longed to be free,

This weight of expectation was crushing to me.

But in music, I found a beautiful song,

My voice soared high, where I truly belonged.

Though dreams were shattered my spirit stayed bright,

For the stage was my haven, a place of pure light.

At twelve years old , a chance knocked at my door but the door was closed in haste,

A father's control, my dreams went to waste.

Yet I held onto hope, through the years I would fight,

For the girl on the stage, who longed for her flight.

The struggle was real, with battles to wage,

As I fought for my worth, stepping out of the cage.

In a cycle of pain, I broke free from the chains,

Finding courage within, dancing through the rains.

Abuse whispered lies, yet truth kept me strong,

In the face of torment, I learned I belong.

Shattered by fear, yet rising again,

The strength of a warrior flows deep in my brain

I stood up for myself, a mother with heart,

Breaking through silence, I played my part.

No longer alone, my future in sight,

With love for my children, I claimed my own right.

Now, I tell my story, through melody and rhyme,

With every note sung, I reclaim my own time.

This ends with me, the cycle is broken,

A legacy of strength in each word that I have spoken.

So here's to the journey, from clouds up above,

To finding my power, my worth, and my love.

I stand in my truth, against all that has been, the face in the clouds is

A testimony of hope, and this ends with me, the win!

Where It All Began

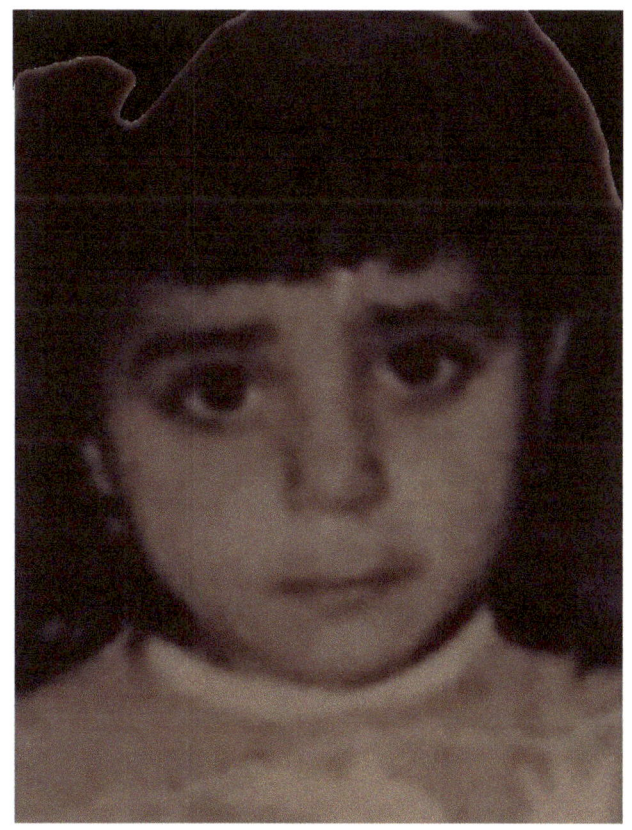

About the Author

Tina Calleri is a survivor, speaker, singer, and advocate whose life embodies the spirit of resilience and renewal. Born in Italy and raised in Canada, her early years were marked by cultural challenges, domestic responsibilities, and the weight of generational expectations. Yet through adversity, Tina found her strength—first in music, then, ultimately, in her own voice.

For over three decades, Tina has nurtured the minds and hearts of young children through flourishing home daycare, where she integrates music, play, and storytelling to cultivate emotional intelligence and confidence. Her professional success as an Early Childhood Specialist is matched by her personal mission: to break cycles of silence and shame, and to empower others—especially women and children—to reclaim their worth.

www.ingramcontent.com/pod-product-compliance
Lightning Source LLC
Chambersburg PA
CBHW051604120626
46551CB00013B/1661